ASTRONOMY

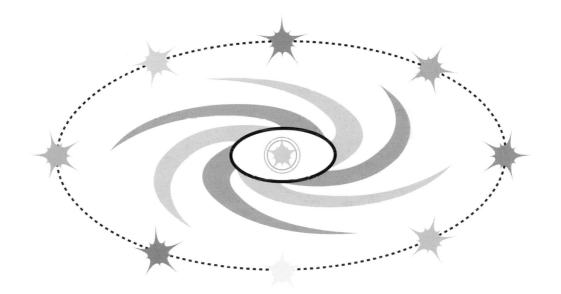

KINGFISHER
NEW YORK

Consultant: Carole Stott

Designed and created by Basher
www.basherworld.com
www.bebo.com/simonbasher

Dedicated to Kas Coleman

Distributed in the U.S. by Macmillan, 175 Fifth Ave., New York, NY 10010
Distributed in Canada by H.B. Fenn and Company Ltd., 34 Nixon Road,
Bolton, Ontario L7E 1W2

Library of Congress Cataloging-in-Publication data has been applied for.

ISBN: 978-0-7534-6290-4

Kingfisher books are available for special promotions and premiums.
For details contact: Special Markets Department, Macmillan,
175 Fifth Avenue, New York, NY 10010.

For more information, please visit www.kingfisherpublications.com

First published in 2009
Printed in Taiwan
10 9 8 7 6 5 4 3
3TR/1009/SHENS/SC/126.6gsm/C

CONTENTS

Introduction   4
The Sun   6
The Solar System   8
Inner Circle   10
Gas Giant Gang   30
Distant Outriders   46
Rising Stars   56
All-Star Crew   72
Local Group   88
Deep Space Gang   100
The Universals   112
Index   124
Glossary   126

Introduction

The Universe/Galileo

Astronomy is the study of everything in the universe, from all the celestial bodies to space itself. From the Greek for "law of the stars" (*astron* means "star" and *nomos* means "law"), it is a science with a wonderful-sounding name, and one that is truly out of this world! It's packed full of planets, stars, galaxies, telescopes, space missions, discoveries, and dreams. When you gaze at the night sky, you are looking at the best story ever told!

Galileo Galilei (1564–1642) was the godfather of modern astronomy. Even though he would have been mind-boggled by the complex and enormous reality of what we know today, this Italian superstar scientist blazed a trail, leaving his mark for all to follow. Galileo stood out because he believed in what he could see with his own eyes. Although the best telescopes of the day allowed him to peer only dimly into the solar system, he even demonstrated that the planets orbited the Sun and not Earth. And 400 years later, we know so much more. But 95 percent of the universe still isn't understood, which means that there is plenty of opportunity to discover some awesome new characters.

The Sun

* Yellow dwarf star halfway through a ten-billion-year life
* Mammoth ball of exploding gas, its heart burns at 27 million °F (15 million °C)
* Its closest star is a puny brown dwarf, 25 trillion mi. (40 trillion km) away

I'm a total star—the center of everything, baby! A fearsome fireball burning 600 million tons of hydrogen every second, I provide light and heat for the orbiting scraps of matter called planets. Holding on to a chunky 99.8 percent of the mass of Solar System, I'm the largest thing in space for light-years around.

I'm a seething mass of anger. At the heart of my boiling cauldron, atoms of hydrogen fuse together to make helium (nuclear fusion), releasing enough energy to blow me to smithereens. But the gravity from my sheer bulk keeps me together. I have a blast, spraying a lethal wind of charged particles and neutrinos into the solar system. Be thankful that your planet is protected by a magnetic shield; otherwise my radioactive winds would finish you off!

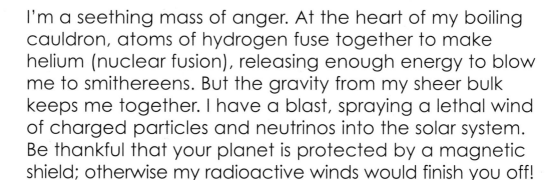

Never look directly at the Sun.

* Size: 864,000 mi. (1.39 million km) across
* Surface temp.: 10,000°F (5,500°C)
* Mass: 333,000 times Earth's

The Sun

The Solar System

* Far-flung family that revolves around a star called the Sun
* This "home" system is in the Orion arm of the Milky Way galaxy
* It takes 225 million years to orbit the galaxy's center

I am a big, happy family that lives in a region of space one million times wider than Earth. The Sun is like a hippo Hula-Hooping through space, creating a graceful and fantastically wide shape. Big Daddy Sun holds almost all of the weight, and his enormous gravity makes the eight planets (with their 166 known moons), three dwarf planets, plus billions of asteroids, comets, meteoroids, and interplanetary dust, spin like a vast whirling tutu around him.

All the main planets circle the Sun, in the same direction, on a flat disk around the Sun's center. Distances between them are immense—Saturn is twice as far from the Sun as its inner neighbor, Jupiter, is. With light zapping along at 186,000 mi. (300,000km)/s, it would be five hours before the farthest members of the family would notice if the Sun was turned off!

Proxima Centauri is the closest star to the Sun and solar system.

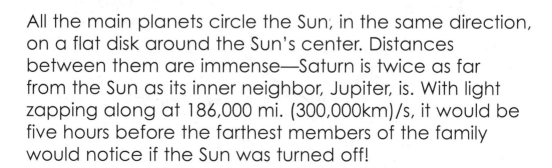

* Age of the solar system: five billion years
* Planets formed: 4.6 million years ago
* Sun's gravity extends: 12.4 million mi. (20 million km)

The Solar System

CHAPTER 1
Inner Circle

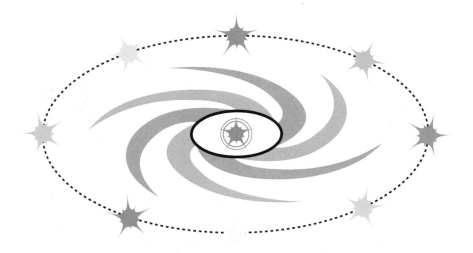

Basking in toasty warmth, these characters orbit closest to the heat engine of the solar system, the Sun. The group's four planets—along with Asteroid Belt—are iron-hearted hard cases with metal cores and rocky exteriors. These rocky rebels used to be hot stuff, but their once-hot liquid centers have cooled and solidified. Only Earth still has active volcanoes burping out molten gas and rock. Tons of high-tech machinery whiz around this neighborhood. Here, too, lies the solar system's only true alien planet— Earth—with its strange inhabitants!

 Mercury

 Venus

 Earth

 Meteorite

 Space Junk

 International Space Station

 The Moon

 Mars

 Mars Rovers

 Asteroid Belt

Mercury
■ Inner Circle

✴ Size: 3,032 mi. (4,879km) across ✴ Temp.: −275–800°F (−170–430°C)
✴ Year: 88 Earth days ✴ Gravity: 0.37 times Earth's
✴ Spin: 58.6 Earth days ✴ Satellites: zero

I can't hang around. There's no time for admiring the view when you live this close to a 27-million-degree fireball. Because I don't stray far from the Sun, you'll only ever catch sight of me around daybreak or nightfall. Like a courier delivering a package, I scoot across the horizon, so the Romans named me after their messenger god.

My fast-paced lifestyle makes it hard for spacecraft to visit me, and only one side of me has yet been photographed. I'm not a pretty sight—my rocky surface is pitted and pockmarked with impact craters. Ever since my hot-blooded youth, my metallic inner core has cooled and shrunk, leaving me with long cliff-face wrinkles. Sunburned by day and fiendishly cold by night, I turn so slowly that it's one Mercury year between sunrise and sunset!

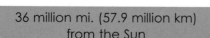
36 million mi. (57.9 million km)
from the Sun

● Top sight: 0.81-mi. (1.3-km)-wide Caloris basin
● Feature: ice lurks in some caves
● Flyby: *Messenger* (2008 onward)

Mercury

Venus
■ Inner Circle

☀ Size: 7,521 mi. (12,104km) across ☀ Temp.: up to 900°F (480°C)
☀ Year: 224.7 Earth days ☀ Gravity: 0.89 times Earth's
☀ Spin: 243 Earth days ☀ Satellites: zero

Bright and shiny, I hang in the sky, a dazzling beauty. My starlike brilliance is caused by the Sun's rays being reflected from my thick yellow clouds—this makes me the most radiant object in the night sky after the Moon. I am named after the Roman goddess of love and appear just before sunrise or just after sunset, so I'm also called the morning star and the evening star.

The thing is, though, I'm a poisonous party pooper. I sulk under an atmospheric blanket of sulfuric acid and carbon dioxide, where the pressure is so great that it could crush a submarine. My parched volcanic surface is chapped. It's hot—really hot and stuffy—as greenhouse gases build up and the Sun's heat cannot escape. Earth creatures, beware, lest the same fate befall your planet!

67.2 million mi. (108.2 million km) from the Sun

● Top sight: Gula Mons volcano
● Shape in the night sky: disk or crescent
● First spacecraft visit: *Mariner 2* (1962)

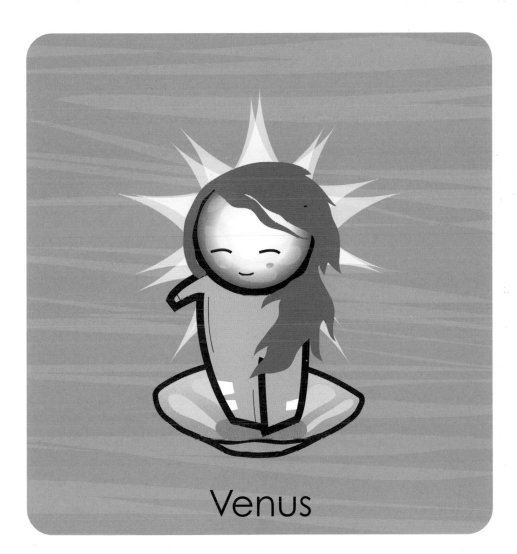

Venus

Earth

■ Inner Circle

✳ Size: 7,926 mi. (12,756km) across   ✳ Temp.: –130–140°F (–90–60°C)
✳ Year: 365.2 Earth days   ✳ Gravity: 32 ft. (9.8m)/s²
✳ Spin: 23.9 hours   ✳ Satellites: one (the Moon)

I'm a true original. Dressed mostly in cool blue, I'm like no other planet in the solar system. Some say that I'm just a big drip, as I'm the only celestial body with surface water. But that's not the only way I'm unique—I'm the birthplace and home of life. With my oxygen, warmth, and liquid-water combo, there's no place like me anywhere else.

I'm a lively orb. Around an inner core, which keeps me rock solid, a twirling outer core of molten iron generates a magnetic current. Then comes a thick layer of simmering mantle rock. The huge plates that make up my thin crust creep around on this glop. I spin fast on my axis, and because I'm tilted at a crazy angle, I have seasons. So for part of the year my northern half leans closer to the Sun, and at other times my southern half is closer.

93 million mi. (149.6 million km)
from the Sun

● Age: 4.6 billion years
● Area of surface water: 73%
● Earth's tilt: 23.5°

Earth

Meteorite

■ Inner Circle

※ Hot-headed space rock that plummets to Earth with a bang
※ A nighttime streaker that lights up the sky
※ Kamikaze kid that comes from debris left in a comet's wake

Look out! Blazing through Earth's atmosphere and smashing into the ground, I can punch a crater in Earth as I crash and burn. To be a meteorite, you can't be any old space rock—you have to make it all the way down. Those of us that burn up before reaching the ground are called meteors or shooting stars. Our main claim to fame is being blamed for wiping out the dinosaurs.

Meteorite

The KT (dino-killing) meteorite sent Earth into a blackout 65 million years ago.

● Largest meteorite found in: Namibia
● Biggest crater: Barringer, Arizona
● Earth's best meteor shower:
    November 12, 1833

Space Junk

✳ An assortment of human-made bits and pieces orbiting Earth
✳ Traveling at high speeds, they are a danger to space traffic
✳ If they enter Earth's atmosphere, they burn up as artificial meteors

Space Junk

Ha-ha! We're free-ee! A mix of spunky escapees, we are the leftovers from 50 years of space missions. We're the fugitives—from globs of nuclear coolant and empty rocket boosters to space gloves. Even tiny flecks of paint can make bullet-style holes in spacecraft as they race around at more than 17,400 mph (28,000km/h). We won't stop for anyone, so stay out of our way!

● Objects bigger than 4 in. (10cm): 10,000
● Objects bigger than 0.08 in. (2mm): 1,000,000
● Oldest space junk: *Vanguard 1* (1958)

The explosion of the *Pegasus* rocket in 1996 added 300,000 more fragments.

International Space Station

☀ Manned satellite made from modules that clip together
☀ Its solar panels twinkle on dark nights as it whizzes overhead
☀ The most extravagant science project . . . EVER!

Cruisin' at 220 mi. (350km) above Earth, I'm like a diamond in the sky. You don't get much more flashy than me. I'm the most expensive thing ever made. My critics say that I'm a big, fat waste of money and that eventually I will become a massive gleaming piece of space junk, but they've missed the point. I'm already a huge recycling project, mostly assembled from rocket boosters bolted together.

Since 2000, my buzzing little space hub has never been empty. The Russian carrier *Soyuz* ferries changes of crew up from Earth. I'm the ultimate space lab—my astronauts investigate how the human body copes with space flight and do dangerous tests on how stuff burns in space!

ISS hosted the first space wedding in 2003.

● Launched: first section in 1998
● Average number of astronauts onboard: three
● Number of orbits around Earth: 15/day

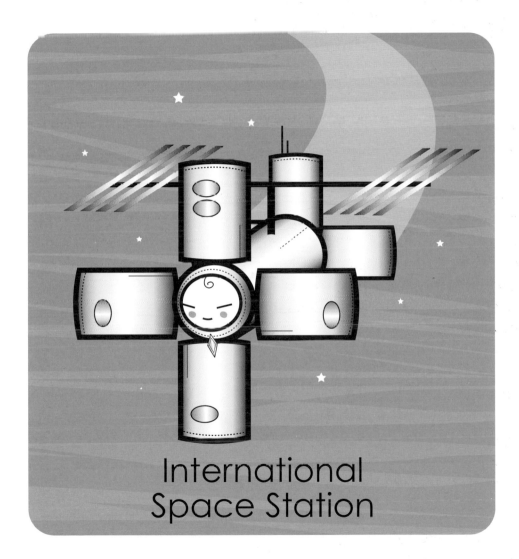

International Space Station

The Moon

■ Inner Circle

✳ Size: 2,159 mi. (3,475km) across
✳ Circles Earth: 27.3 Earth days
✳ Spin: 27.3 Earth days
✳ Temp.: −270–230°F (−170–110°C)
✳ Gravity: 0.16 times Earth's
✳ Volume: 0.02 times Earth's

I have the biggest and most luminous face in the night sky, but my splendor is only reflected—having no light of my own, my powdery surface bounces the Sun's rays onto Earth. I'm dead, so it's like having the volume on mute. With no wind to blow dust, the footprints of the astronauts who walked across my terrain will stay preserved forever.

Almost identical in age and makeup to Earth, I'm a chip off the old block, formed when a Mars-size asteroid hit Earth. Like dancers, we turn in sync, so the same side of me is always facing Earth. Half of me is always illuminated by the Sun, and as I orbit Earth, different amounts of my bright side can be seen—this cycle from new moon to full moon and back gives Earth a gentle rhythm. As my gravity tugs on Earth's oceans, it creates the tides.

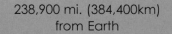

238,900 mi. (384,400km) from Earth

● Top sight: Bailly crater (180 mi. or 290km across)
● Number of moonquakes: 1,500 per year
● Drift from Earth: 1 in. (3cm) per year

The Moon

Mars
■ Inner Circle

✴ Size: 4,220 mi. (6,792km) across ✴ Temp.: −165–32°F (−110–0°C)
✴ Year: 687 Earth days ✴ Gravity: 0.37 times Earth's
✴ Spin: 24.6 hours ✴ Satellites: two

Hanging in the night sky like a bloodshot eye, I'm a rusty old warhorse, named after the Roman god of war. Iron minerals give me my reddish inflamed look. I was once a delightful planet with water flowing over my rocky surface, but these days I'm a chilly, hard-bitten world of dead volcanoes and dry rift valleys. Dust devils and tornadoes swirl across the landscape, but because my atmosphere is now very thin, there is little strength to them.

At one-half the size of Earth, I don't have the mass to hold onto my surface gases forever, or the volume to fuel a fire at my core to keep me warm. Dried riverbeds and polar caps of dry ice are the only traces of my suppressed youth. Earthlings are fascinated by the idea that I could be home to Martians, yet despite all their probing, there's still no sign.

141.6 million mi. (227.9 million km)
from the Sun

● Top sight: Olympus Mons volcano
● First spacecraft visit: *Viking 1* (1976)
● Moons: Phobos and Deimos

Mars

Mars Rovers
■ Inner Circle

✹ Six-wheeled robotic twins named *Spirit* and *Opportunity*
✹ Solar-powered duo that poke their noses into Martian soil
✹ They have asteroids named in honor of their great work

We're a pair of pioneers, making tracks across a distant planet. We come bristling with cameras (our "roving" eyes), magnets for collecting dust particles, and high-tech scientific equipment for analyzing Martian rocks and minerals. We arrived in 2004, on opposite sides of the planet, expecting only a short and busy life—but tenacious and terrier-like, we've just kept on trucking, becoming one of NASA's biggest success stories.

It's a perilous job, and there's no one who can repair us if things go wrong—if anything damages our solar panels, which power us, it's game over. We suffer from a nighttime freeze and hunker down over the winter to protect our delicate electronics. We've gone through all sorts of hardships, and we keep on going courageously!

A nine-year-old Russian girl named Sofi Collis chose their names.

● Weight: 385 lbs. (180kg) each
● Height: 4.9 ft. (1.5m)
● Top speed: 2 in. (50mm)/s

Mars Rovers

Asteroid Belt

■ Inner Circle

✳ Jumble of rocks hanging around between Mars and Jupiter
✳ Chunks of space debris that never got together as planets
✳ One of them, Ceres, was promoted to a dwarf planet in 2006

We're a bunch of rockers. Jagged-shaped pieces of rock, we jostle around on an elliptical path, forming a gappy wall that separates the Inner Circle and the Gas Giant Gang. Jupiter's bullying gravitational pull has shepherded us into this no man's land in space. Because of Jupiter's gravity, we're always crashing into one another and shattering, so we've never been able to join together to form a planet. We can't even smooth over the gaps and make an unbroken band, as Jupiter enjoys flinging us into wider, erratic orbits or sucking us into its own.

Some of us, called near Earth asteroids (NEAs), are more "nasty 'roids" than asteroids, because the orbits of these bad guys send them tumbling on a course dangerously close to Earth. So, watch out!

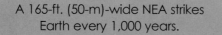

A 165-ft. (50-m)-wide NEA strikes Earth every 1,000 years.

● Number of asteroids more than 0.62 mi. (1km) wide: 40,000
● Largest asteroid: Ceres (585 mi. or 940km wide)
● First landing on an asteroid: *Eros* (2001)

Asteroid Belt

CHAPTER 2
Gas Giant Gang

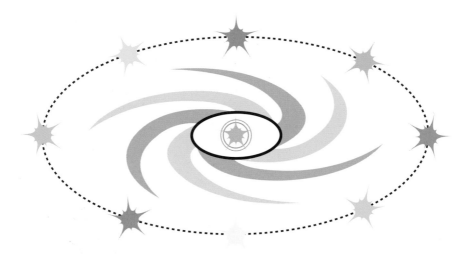

Life's a gas for these lords of the solar system. The four imposing outer planets, made of vast amounts of hydrogen, comprise—along with their enormous moons—more than 99 percent of the mass of everything that orbits the Sun. These planets are the only ones you'd spot from outside the solar system. Powerful atmospheric forces keep this gang of ring-wearing buccaneers buzzing. The great pressure created by their layered clouds crushes hydrogen until it forms liquid seas buried deep in the haze.

Jupiter

Jupiter's Moons

Saturn

Cassini-Huygens

Titan

Uranus

Neptune

Jupiter
■ Gas Giant Gang

✳ Size: 88,846 mi. (142,984km) across ✳ Temp.: −255−−165°F (−160−−110°C)
✳ Year: 4,331 Earth days ✳ Gravity: 2.31 times Earth's
✳ Spin: 9.9 hours ✳ Satellites: 63 known

I coulda been a contender—a real star—but instead I'm just the biggest planet. I'm absolutely gigantic, made almost entirely of hydrogen gas (plus a little helium, too), and I have a system of moons orbiting me. If I'd had just a little bit more beef, I would have burst into life as a bright and wonderful star. Oh, for a few extra pounds!

Even though I'm called the King of the Solar System, I'm still angry. I spin rapidly, whirling my atmosphere into thick bands of double-decker clouds that give me my coffee-and-cream appearance. There's nothing genteel about these cloud banks—inside them, winds blow at 260 mph (420km/h), whisking up enormous storms. My most famous blemish—the Great Red Spot—is a storm three times bigger than Earth that's been raging since the 1600s.

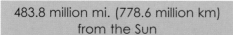
483.8 million mi. (778.6 million km)
from the Sun

● Top sight: Great Red Spot
● Latest spacecraft visit: New Horizons (2007)
● Mass: 318 times Earth's

Jupiter

Jupiter's Moons
Gas Giant Gang

* The 63 moons that orbit Jupiter are like a mini solar system
* The largest are Ganymede, Callisto, Europa, and Io
* Galileo was the first to publish his observations in 1610

We're a bunch of burly brothers and sisters called the Galilean moons or, sometimes, the Jovian moons, after the Roman god Jove (AKA Jupiter). And what a jovial bunch we are! Well, *some* of us are . . .

Io is the grump with a nonstop upset stomach—she's so close to her master's powerful gravity that her innards are wrenched this way and that, constantly spewing out smelly volcanoes of sulfur. Smaller than Io, Europa is a world of calm covered in a smooth crust of solid ice, with a warm, salty ocean 15 mi. (25km) below the surface. Ganymede is the solar system's largest moon and the only one with a magnetic field—and a personality to match! Poor old Callisto's a dead world whose craggy ancient landscape has been peppered by meteorites.

Galileo's observations helped prove that Earth wasn't the center of the universe.

* Also spotted by: Simon Marius (1610)
* Ganymede's diameter: 3,270 mi. (5,262km)
* Visited by: *Galileo* probe (1995)

Jupiter's Moons

Saturn
■ Gas Giant Gang

✳ Size: 74,898 mi. (120,536km) across ✳ Temperature: −290°F (−180°C)
✳ Year: 10,747 Earth days ✳ Gravity: 0.9 times Earth's
✳ Spin: 10.7 hours ✳ Satellites: at least 60

Forget about the charms of lovely Venus: I am the pearl of the solar system. I grace the skies dressed in demure creams and browns, with elegant bands around my middle and a six-sided crown of clouds floating over my north pole. Electric blue lights play around both my poles, a lot like Earth's northern and southern lights.

Like a skilled Hula-Hoop dancer, I spin a number of rings around my middle. Made up of everything from dust to car-size boulders of ice and rock, these flat rings are kept neatly in place by the gravity of my shepherd moons. My dazzling hoops are very thin (about 164 ft. or 50m) and can be seen stretching out more than 155,000 mi. (250,000km). I'm made of such lightweight gases that I'd float on water like a giant inflatable ball (if you could find a big enough tank)!

890.7 million mi. (1.4 billion km) from the Sun

- Discoverer (rings): Galileo (1610)
- Cloud-top wind speeds: 1,200 mph (2,000km/h)
- First spacecraft visit: *Pioneer 11* (1979)

Saturn

Cassini-Huygens
■ Gas Giant Gang

✴ A pair of heavy-hitting space probes on a mission to Saturn
✴ Cassini-Huygens will glide around the planet 74 times
✴ Their sharp eyes have spotted hurricanes and new moons

We're a pair of highfliers who run rings around the solar system. Cassini's the chunky one who does all the talking, and Huygens (say "High-gens") is the sassy sidekick who's done all the daring stuff. With 1,630 electronic gizmos, 22,000 wire links, and more than 9 ft. (14km) of cables between us, we've made history as the most complicated space probes—and the first to go into orbit around Saturn!

We're on one of the trickiest-ever missions—to study Saturn's rings, magnetic field, and atmosphere, plus seven of its moons. On January 14, 2005, little Huygens became the first human-made thing to explore Saturn's biggest moon, Titan. It punched through thick, swirling clouds, withstanding blistering 32,400°F (18,000°C) temperatures, to give us knockout pictures of Titan's creepy methane lakes.

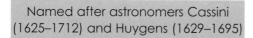
Named after astronomers Cassini (1625–1712) and Huygens (1629–1695)

● Launch date: October 15, 1997
● Size: 22 ft. (6.7m) high and 13 ft. (4m) wide
● Time for signals to reach Earth: 1.5 hours

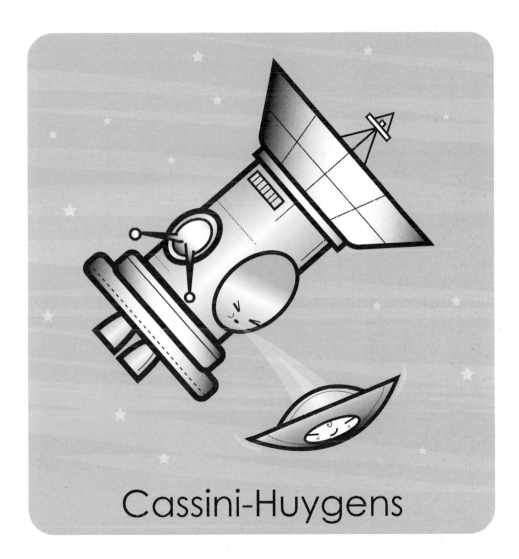

Cassini-Huygens

Titan
■ Gas Giant Gang

* Saturn's largest moon, a colossus measuring 3,200 mi. (5,150km) across
* A 125-mi. (200-km)-deep haze covers its delightful surface
* Titan's Earthlike features get astronomers hot under the collar

As the solar system's second-largest moon, I am even bigger than Mercury! I am also the only moon with a permanent atmosphere, which engulfs me in a reddish haze. My atmosphere, made of methane, is thicker than Earth's. It's so thick that humans could swim through it, high up above my solid surface.

I managed to hide my secrets from prying eyes until 2005, when the Huygens lander crashed through my cloud tops to reveal an amazing world. My surface has a few craters, some sand dunes, and many lakes—and it looks . . . well, a lot like Earth! I even have wind, rain, and seasonal weather, but it's much, much colder here than on Earth. Something unknown is recycling the methane in my atmosphere. Could it be alien microbes and the beginnings of life?

Surface pressure would feel like being at the bottom of a swimming pool.

● Discoverer: Christiaan Huygens (1655)
● Visited by: *Cassini-Huygens* (2005)
● Temperature: −288°F (−178°C)

Titan

Uranus

Gas Giant Gang

- Size: 31,763 mi. (51,118km) across
- Year: 30,589 Earth days
- Spin: 17.2 hours
- Temperature: –345°F (–210°C)
- Gravity: 0.87 times Earth's
- Satellites: 27

I'm the second-smallest member of the Gas Giant Gang, and I've taken a few knocks in my life. With a name like mine, I've been the "butt" of many jokes, yet my correct pronunciation is not "your-anus" but "you-ranus"! Another big blow to my ego came early on in my history when a humongous collision knocked me over. I now spin on my side, with my axis at right angles to all the other planets.

Because of this odd orientation, my poles take turns facing away from the Sun for 21 years at a time. I cook up huge spring storms that send clouds of crystalline methane racing at 260 mph (420km/h) around my aquamarine face. Like all Gas Giants, I have a ring system. However, my set of 11 rings is very thin and wasn't spotted until I was photographed up close by the *Kuiper* probe in 1977.

1.8 billion mi. (2.9 billion km) from the Sun

- Discoverer: William Herschel (1781)
- Visited by: *Voyager 2* (1986)
- Thickness of rings: as little as 33 ft. (10m)

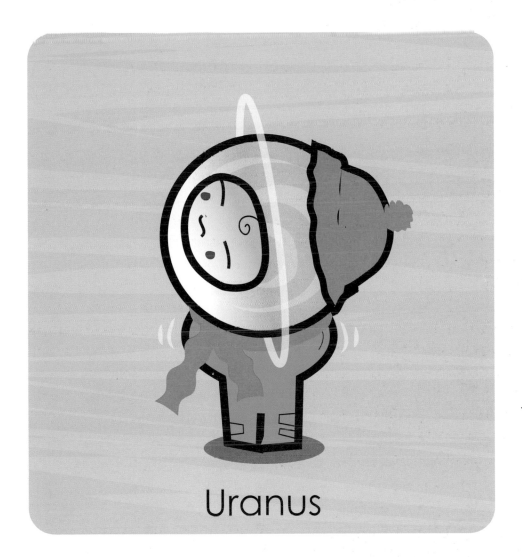

Uranus

Neptune
■ Gas Giant Gang

✷ Size: 30,775 mi. (49,528km) across ✷ Temperature: –345°F (–210°C)
✷ Year: 59,800 Earth days ✷ Gravity: 1.1 times Earth's
✷ Spin: 16.1 hours ✷ Satellites: 13

Wrapped in a cool blue shroud, I'm the solar system's king of bling. Pure white ammonia clouds zip across my azure-colored face—racing along at 1,550 mph (2,500km/h), they're the speediest clouds in the solar system. Under this cloak lies an ocean of boiling methane, and inside this, diamonds crystallize. For real, dude!

As the farthest true planet from the Sun, I'm most definitely "out there." Well, I was the first planet to be located by mathematical prediction rather than direct observation. Being stormy, I'm prone to dark moods, and for 20 years, a giant tornado called the Great Dark Spot spun across my southern hemisphere. Along with my twin, Uranus, I'm a bit of an ice giant, as my cloud-top temperatures are some of the chilliest in the solar system.

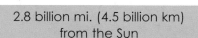
2.8 billion mi. (4.5 billion km)
from the Sun

● Discoverers: Urbain Le Verrier, John
    Couch Adams, Johann Galle (1846)
● Visited by: *Voyager 2* (1989)
● Its moon orbits in the opposite direction.

Neptune

CHAPTER 3
Distant Outriders

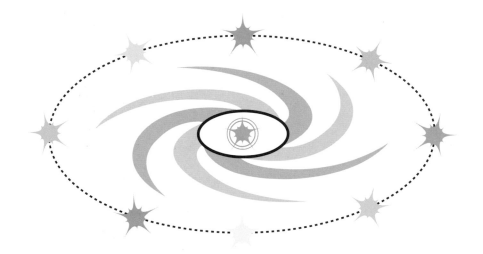

This troupe is a ragtag collection of oddballs left out in the cold. Excluded from the main planets, the dwarfs—Pluto and Eris—live life in the slow lane, taking hundreds of years to orbit the Sun. These two mavericks travel on a path that tilts at a streamlined angle compared with the solar system's other planets. The probes *New Horizons* and the *Voyagers* boldy venture where none have gone before, like ambassadors from Earth. Out here, on the fringes of the solar system, comets are stockpiled in Kuiper Belt and Oort Cloud, waiting to pelt the inner planets.

Pluto

Eris

New Horizons

Voyagers

Kuiper Belt

Oort Cloud

Halley's Comet

Pluto

■ Distant Outriders

* Size: 1,485 mi. (2,390km) across
* Year: 90,588 Earth days
* Spin: 6.4 Earth days

* Temperature: –380°F (–230°C)
* Gravity: 0.06 times Earth's
* Satellites: three

After being thrown out of the main planets' club in 2006, I was demoted to a mere dwarf planet. I orbit the Sun face-to-face with my twin, Charon (say "Karon"). Out here, the Sun looks like a pinhead, and only a smidgen of its life-giving warmth reaches our frozen worlds. Sometimes we nip inside Neptune's orbit and get closer to the Sun for 20 years at a time.

Pluto

3.7 billion mi. (5.9 billion km) from the Sun

● Pluto's discoverer: Clyde Tombaugh (1930)
● Charon's discoverer: James Christy (1978)
● *New Horizons* encounter: 2015

Distant Outriders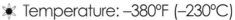

- ☀ Size: 1,550 mi. (2,500km) across
- ☀ Year: 205,000 Earth days
- ☀ Spin: unknown

- ☀ Temperature: −380°F (−230°C)
- ☀ Gravity: 0.08 times Earth's
- ☀ Satellites: one

Eris

Twice as far from the Sun as Pluto, my discovery created havoc in the world of astronomy. Icy, distant, and mysterious, I'm the largest of the newish group of dwarf planets. Before getting my official name from the Greek goddess of discord and strife, I was known as 2003 UB313. I have a partner in crime— a companion moon named Dysnomia, after the Greek god of lawlessness!

- ● First spotted: 2003
- ● Discoverers; M. E. Brown, C. A. Trujillo, D. L. Rabinowitz
- ● Nicknames: Xena, Planet X

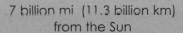

7 billion mi. (11.3 billion km) from the Sun

New Horizons
■ Distant Outriders

※ A spacecraft boldly going where none has gone before
※ Will pass within 6,200 mi. (10,000km) of Pluto and 16,800 mi. (27,000km) of Charon
※ Speed freak with the record for the fastest-ever launch

Streaking into the bottomless blackness of space, I'm the size and shape of a grand piano. On my way to Kuiper Belt, I'm hoping to get a good look at Pluto, which has never been visited by a space probe. I'm also keeping my eyes peeled for any ring systems or undiscovered moons. This far from the Sun, I need an onboard nuclear power plant to keep me going!

New Horizons

Carries some ashes of Pluto's discoverer, Clyde Tombaugh

● Launch date: January 19, 2006
● Pluto encounter: July 14, 2015
● Takeoff speed: 36,258 mph (58,352km/h)

- ☀ Sibling team of probes launched in 1977
- ☀ These sightseers have visited the most planets and moons
- ☀ Both carry a "golden record" with pictures and sounds of Earth

Voyagers

We are world-beating brothers from another decade. After visiting Jupiter and Saturn, *Voyager 1* is heading for outer space. Now more than twice as far from the Sun as Pluto, it's the farthest-flung piece of equipment ever made! Then there's *Voyager 2*— the only probe to do a grand tour of all the Gas Giant Gang planets. We have until only 2020 before our systems will blink out.

- ● Distance from the Sun: more than 7.4 billion mi. (12 billion km)
- ● *Voyager 1* speed: 62,097 mph (99,936km/h)
- ● Time for signals to reach Earth: 14 hours

Voyager 2 photos show that our solar system is squashed, not round!

Kuiper Belt
■ Distant Outriders

✳ A bunch of shivering, icy bodies, starting at Neptune's orbit
✳ About 20 times wider than scrawny Asteroid Belt
✳ Its largest-known members, Pluto and Eris, are dwarf planets

Our name rhymes with *viper*, and you can bet your snakeskin boots that we live up to it. Banished far away from the comfort of the Sun by the gravity of the Gas Giants, we form a fence of frosty missiles. We include many small and irregularly shaped bodies with a similar makeup to the dwarf planets. The much larger and more round objects, which also inhabit this zone, are called plutoids.

Kuiper Belt

Discovered by David Jewitt
and Jane Luu in 1992

● Number of KB objects: more than 100,000
● Largest member: Eris
● Width of belt: more than 3.7 billion mi.
  (6 billion km)

* A storehouse for long-period comets
* Astronomers have figured out its position from comets' flight paths
* A thousand times farther away than Kuiper Belt

Oort Cloud

I'm a spherical cloud of comets around the entire edge of the solar system. Blacker than coal and colder than a freezer, I have never been directly observed. My dirty balls of rock and ice have a split personality—they're quiet and unassuming in the far-flung regions of space, but once past Jupiter and warmed by the Sun, they grow tails of water and carbon-dioxide vapor.

* Discoverer: Jan Oort (1950)
* Width: 1.6 ly (light-years)
* Comets more than 60 mi. (100km) wide: 35,000

Hale-Bopp is the most famous long-period comet.

53

Halley's Comet
■ Distant Outriders

※ Peanut-shaped comet that visits Earth every 75–76 years
※ Its spectacular blazing tail stretches out for more than 60 mi. (100km)
※ Debris left in Halley's wake causes two meteor showers each year

Hurtling in from the cold wastelands of Kuiper Belt on an elliptical path, I am the most famous of all the comets. Neither the brightest nor the most glamorous, my celebrity status was won when I became the first to be recognized as periodic. In other words, I'm on an endless loop around the Sun.

Passing by Earth so often, I'm known as a short-period comet. I've witnessed a lot of Earth's history. I showed up just before William the Conqueror met King Harold at the Battle of Hastings in 1066—Willy viewed me as a sign of good fortune (he won the battle, by the way). I graced the skies in 1986 and will visit again in 2061. Most people will see me only once in their lifetime, so make sure you get a good look. I've got to shoot!

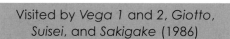

Visited by *Vega 1* and *2*, *Giotto*, *Suisei*, and *Sakigake* (1986)

● Orbit predicted by: Edmund Halley (1758)
● Size: 9 mi. (15km) long and 4.6 mi. (7.5km) wide
● Average speed: 43.84 mi. (70.56km)/s

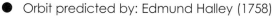

Halley's Comet

CHAPTER 4
Rising Stars

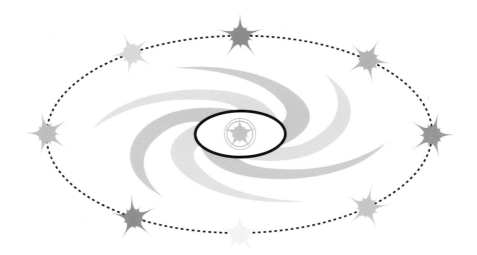

It's all glitter and celebrity as this bunch of up-and-coming young bucks graduates from Star Birth Nebula and sets out on the road to stardom. Each one tries to get nuclear fusion reactions going inside its core (to power its radiant brilliance) and to strike a balance between its explosive energy and crushing gravity. But the life of a Rising Star is full of danger—it might burn too brightly and blast itself apart or be blown away by its stronger classmates. But should it start to shine, its destiny is decided by the amount of material it has.

Constellation

Star Birth Nebula

Open Cluster

Brown Dwarf

Red Dwarf

Alpha Centauri

Extrasolar Planet

Supergiant

Constellation

Rising Stars

✳ A pattern formed by bright stars in the night sky
✳ Different ones can be seen at different times of the year
✳ Its brightest star is almost always called the alpha star

With no TV to entertain them at night, it's no wonder that ancient astronomers saw all their favorite stories played out in the night sky above them. Babylonian and Egyptian stargazers found giant scorpions, charging bulls, and men with horses' bodies in the patterns of stars.

My outline shape is still used, although these days my constellation name refers to a region of the sky, like countries on a world map. Even though my stars look like they are close to one another, it's a trick of the eye—the stars that make up my pattern may be in completely separate parts of the galaxy, so my shape makes sense only from Earth. All these stars are on journeys, but since they're so unimaginably distant, they move by minuscule amounts in the sky and appear rooted in position.

Smaller patterns within a constellation are called asterisms.

● Number of constellations: 88
● Largest constellation: Hydra (Snake)
● Smallest constellation: Crux (Southern Cross)

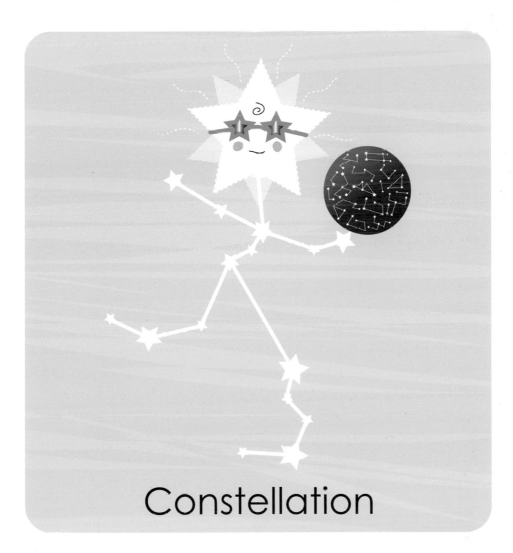

Constellation

Star Birth Nebula
Rising Stars

* A clouded region of space that is a nursery for new stars
* Infrared light exposes young stars hidden by thick clouds
* Stars can hang around for 100 million years before bursting into life

Nebulae like me are the universe's coldest, darkest, and most secret places. Behind our heavy curtains of dust and gas, we go about our mysterious work. We are the places where new stars are born—and, like magicians, we clear our haze to reveal young stars of all masses forming inside.

Thousands of times more massive than the Sun, I am made of hydrogen and helium, as well as traces of heavier metal elements and a smattering of complex carbon chemicals. My clouds are uneven and lumpy, like cold mashed potatoes, and come in weird and wonderful shapes. My tightly packed clumpy parts start to form swirling balls of gas when shaken up by nearby supernovae or passing stars. These gassy balls fall in on themselves, under their own gravity, to become stars.

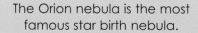
The Orion nebula is the most famous star birth nebula.

* A supergiant forms in: 20,000 years
* A Sunlike star forms in: 100 million years
* Brightest in the night sky: Orion nebula

Star Birth Nebula

Open Cluster
Rising Stars

※ A small gang of competitive young stars, all out for themselves
※ This brood forms collapsing clumps inside a star birth nebula
※ These few thousand stars are all formed at the same time

We're a loosely knit bunch who formed together inside a star birth nebula. There, we learned how to be starlets, but some of us graduated before the rest. As it is for all up-and-coming talent, the early years are tough. Star birth nebulae form stars with different masses that may go on to become violent supergiants or docile brown dwarfs.

Heavier stars burst onto the scene and hog the limelight, while the lighter ones struggle to get going. Some brutish young stars blast others apart with jets of superheated gas and high-energy x-rays, like stellar blowtorches. The lighter stars are the losers in these fights and many die. As things settle down and we all start shining brightly, we blow away the remnants of the cloudy star birth nebula with a fresh solar wind streaming from our shiny new cores.

Pleiades (the Seven Sisters) is the most famous open cluster.

● Open clusters in the Milky Way: 100–1,000
● Most massive (Milky Way): Westerlund 1
● Average age: more than ten million years

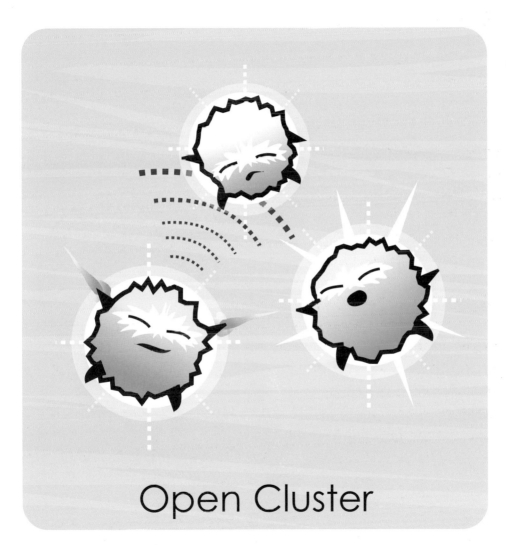

Open Cluster

Brown Dwarf
Rising Stars

✳ Dimwitted failed star, without the mass to shine brightly
✳ No hoper who doesn't heat up enough for nuclear reactions
✳ Timid brown dwarfs are 20 to 80 times heavier than Jupiter

I'm not dazzlingly brilliant, but characters like me are the missing links between stars and planets. The runts of the star birth nebula litter, we simply lacked enough gassy matter to kick-start nuclear fusion in our cores. Shy and retiring, we still manage to glow weakly. Don't take me lightly—many times heavier than the most giant planets, I can cause nearby stars to wobble.

Brown Dwarf

Teide 1(1995) was the first brown dwarf discovered.

● Typical brown dwarf: Gliese 229B
● Distance from Earth: 18.8 ly
● Temperature: 1,800–3,600°F (1,000–2,000°C)

Red Dwarf
Rising Stars

* A starlet weighing less than 50 percent of the Sun's mass
* Together these characters make up a lot of the Milky Way's bulk
* These tiny guys are too dim to be seen with the naked eye

Red Dwarf

I might not be the most impressive type of star, but I have strength in numbers. As your galaxy's most common star, this age belongs to me! I'm never heavier than a yellow dwarf, which itself isn't that large a beast, so I shine only faintly. Proxima Centauri, the closest star to the Sun, is a red dwarf, and it orbits a very unusual double-star system called Alpha Centauri.

- Orbit of Alpha Centauri: one million years
- Proxima Centauri: 4.2 ly away
- Temperature: 4,500–6,300°F (2,500–3,500°C)

Red dwarf Gliese 581 is orbited by an intriguing Earthlike exoplanet.

Alpha Centauri
Rising Stars

- The closest stellar system to the Sun, it's visible from Earth
- A triple-star system made up of two yellow dwarfs and a red dwarf
- A possible safe haven for humans in the distant future

I'm a bit of an oddball. While I look like a single blob in Earth's night sky, I'm actually a system of three stars. Alpha Centauri A is a little bigger and brighter than the Sun, while Alpha Centauri B is a little smaller and dimmer. Because the two of us are tightly bound together, our combined light makes us the third-brightest star in the sky. Our third member, a red dwarf named Proxima Centauri, is farther away and, being dull, adds little to our spectacle.

Astronomers think I may support terrestrial planets and, because my principal star is a yellow dwarf—like the Sun—that I might be habitable. Because I'm the Sun's closest neighbor, sci-fi writers like to think I'll make a new home for humankind when the Sun finally dies. The problem is, I'm more than four light-years away from Earth!

Also known as Rigil Kentaurus, which sounds like a movie star!

- Distance from the Sun: 4.2 ly
- Constellation: Centaurus
- Time for space probe to get there: 70,000 years

Alpha Centauri

Extrasolar Planet

Rising Stars

✳ A mysterious planet belonging to a far-flung star
✳ Astronomers hunt excitedly for planets like this
✳ Also called an exoplanet, this could be home to alien life

I'm a speck of gold dust! Planets like me orbit far-off stars and are a kind of Holy Grail for astronomers. We've been playing hide-and-seek with them since the 1800s. Highly elusive, we conceal ourselves in the glare of the stars that we orbit, which makes us tricky to spot. Astronomers look for stars that both "wink," as a planet passes in front of them, and "wobble," as a planet's gravity tugs on them.

Planet hunters mostly find portly, Jupiter-size planets with these methods. But in 2007, up popped Gliese 581d, a planet a mere five times the size of Earth. Excitingly, it's in the warm habitable zone, neither too hot nor too cold for liquid water (and perhaps life) to exist. They don't know whether it's dry, like Mars, sultry, like Venus, or a "Goldilocks" planet that's "just right," like Earth.

OGLE-2005-BLG-390Lb is the most Earthlike extrasolar yet discovered.

● Gliese 581d discoverer: S. Udry (2007)
● Gliese 581d distance from Earth: 20.4 ly
● Number of extrasolar planets: more than 300

Extrasolar Planet

Supergiant
Rising Stars

* Troublemaker who burns in bright white, blue, or red colors
* These bad guys burn at 36 million °F (20 million °C) for 10–50 million years
* The universe's first population of stars was made up of these

Live fast, die young, and go out with a bang—that's my motto! I'm one of the monster stars of the universe, regularly between ten and 70 times more massive than the Sun (and the superheavies are 500 times bigger!). And I burn thousands of times brighter.

Like enormous stellar foundries, my ancestors produced most of the iron and other heavy elements in the universe. Blazing at such scorchingly hot temperatures, I can eat up all the heavier elements, but this greedy streak means that life's over in a flash. My fierce nuclear reactions create howling radioactive gales that constantly blast away my outer layers. Like a petulant hothead, one day I'll explode in the most terrifying cataclysm in the universe—called a supernova.

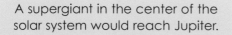

A supergiant in the center of the solar system would reach Jupiter.

* On average, ten times a red giant's size
* Up to 100,000 times the Sun's brightness
* Famous supergiant: Betelgeuse

Supergiant

CHAPTER 5

All-Star Crew

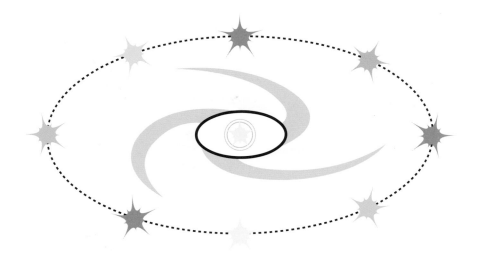

Having run low on hydrogen, this group of well-established stars searches for new fuels to stoke up their nuclear fires. But the ultimate question is how they'll leave the stage— will they end by showering a colorful planetary nebula, bow out gracefully as a dwarf, or blow out in spectacular supernova style? In truth, there's no choice involved—it's all about mass, and the giant stars have very big ideas compared with the more modestly sized ones. But this isn't the end—older, wiser stars know that there is life after death as one of the universe's strangest objects.

Sirius

Betelgeuse

Cat's Eye Nebula

White Dwarf

Supernova

Neutron Star

Black Hole

Supernova
Remnant

Sirius
All-Star Crew

* The brightest star in Earth's night sky, also called the Dog Star
* A double-star system in the constellation of Canis Major
* It's 230 million years old—don't ask for its age in dog years!

I'm the top dog and come as two for the price of one! The ancient Greeks believed that my appearance in the sky brought about the "dog days" of summer—a time when crops (and people) wilted in the breezeless heat. Seen from Earth, I'm almost twice as bright as any other star in the sky (besides the Sun).

My secret is that, like Alpha Centauri and many other stars, I'm a double-star system. I have Sirius A, which is big and shiny, and a hangdog companion, Sirius B, which is tiny and dull. Orbiting each other so closely, we must have formed at the same time. Life has been "ruff" for Sirius B (called the Pup). Because it had more mass at the start and burned much faster, it finished up as a white dwarf. Every dog has its day, and now it's Sirius A's time!

The ancient Greeks saw Sirius as a two-headed dog.

* Discoverer: Alvan Graham Clark (1862)
* Distance from Earth: 8.6 ly
* Temperature: 45,000°F (25,000°C)

Sirius

Betelgeuse
All-Star Crew

* A red supergiant, pronounced "beetle juice" by some people
* Second-brightest star in the constellation of Orion after Rigel
* One of the biggest stars known to humankind

Call a doctor! I'm swelling up and running a temperature of 6,500°F (3,600°C)! Oh no! This is just how red giants kick the bucket. My problem is certainly not old age. At only ten million years old, I'm a mere baby star.

I've lived fast, guzzling my fuel at a tremendous rate. When stars like me run out of hydrogen in our cores, we start using the supplies that are in our outer atmospheres. This sends huge shells of burning hydrogen racing through our bodies and makes us balloon outward. Once all the hydrogen is gone, we usually shrink back and start on our supply of helium. This spells the end for Sunlike stars, but heavies like me are different—we can do this cycle over and over again. So there's a little more life left in me before my supernova sendoff in 1,000 years or so.

Its supernova explosion will appear brighter than the Moon in daylight!

* Distance from Earth: 425 ly
* Size: 650 Suns across
* Brightness: 60,000 times the Sun's

Betelgeuse

Cat's Eye Nebula

All-Star Crew

* A planetary nebula in the constellation of Draco
* Beautiful cloud formation with a dying star at its center
* Its complex cocoon shape suggests a double-star system

With dignity and elegance, I show how modestly sized stars can leave the stage gracefully. When the glory years are over and the final fandango of the red giant period is drawing to a close, it is stars with less than eight times the Sun's mass that become planetary nebulae. Unlike showoff supernovae, we don't go out in a messy explosion but give one of the most awesome sights in the night sky.

My show begins when a red giant starts up nuclear reactions in shells around its core. The radiation blows away matter from the outer atmosphere, creating clouds of encircling gas. Excited by the radiation, these rings glow in magnificent colors. With stellar winds pushing the gas, the performance rarely lasts for more than 10,000 years. At the end, I will bow out as a teeny white dwarf.

62,000-mph (100,000-km/h) winds rage inside the nebula in concentric patterns.

* Discoverer: William Herschel (1786)
* Distance from Earth: 3,300 ly
* Other planetary nebulae include: Helix

Cat's Eye Nebula

White Dwarf
All-Star Crew

✴ A star with the same mass as the Sun but that has run out of gas
✴ Superhot at first, it ultimately turns into a dead, cold star
✴ It's no fool but is one of the densest objects in the universe

I'm what is left after a giant star has given its all. I am part of a degenerate crowd, according to astronomers. I think they're a little too "dwarfist" for my liking. After a lifetime of providing heat, light, and heavy elements for the universe, we demand a little more respect! Besides, I am the core star of a planetary nebula.

I cool and fade when my nuclear fires shut down. There's no energy to keep me from falling in under my own gravity, so I collapse. This is an ultraslow process that ends up making me superdense. There is a limit to how much I can shrink, though, because of the repulsion between my atoms' electrons. If what's left is more than one-and-a-half times the Sun's mass, after hundreds of millions of years I'll become an invisible, cold black dwarf.

A teaspoon of a white dwarf would weigh more than a 4x4 car!

● Discoverers: Henry Norris Russell, Edward Charles Pickering, Williamina Fleming
● Average density: $1 \times 10^9 kg/m^3$
● Stars ending life as white dwarfs: 90%

White Dwarf

Supernova
All-Star Crew

* The biggest explosion in the universe, when a giant star dies
* Supernovae trigger star formations in nearby star birth nebulae
* This superstar's core survives as a neutron star or black hole

A supernova is sensational! It's the last thing that happens to a supergiant star when it fizzles out of fuel and can't keep the nuclear fires at its core burning. I'm one of these stupendous somethings, and bowing out with no fuss isn't for me. When blowing our tops, we celebrate the life of our stars with the biggest fireworks in the universe and wind up with a bang that shines 500 times brighter than the Sun.

We're so fierce that we can outshine a galaxy for several months before fading to black, but it's only the massive stars that go out so spectacularly. We occur when the core of a massive star shuts down. The force of gravity caused by the star's mass overpowers all the repelling interatomic forces. The core collapses in on itself with such energy that it hurls the star's contents across space!

Supernova explosions are expected to increase in the Milky Way.

* Most recently observed: 1987A (1987)
* Occurs in the Milky Way: every 50 years
* Speed of core collapse: 43,500 mi. (70,000km)/s

Supernova

Neutron Star

All-Star Crew

✳ The leftover core after a supernova explosion
✳ With a solid crust of iron, this dude looks like a pinball in space
✳ Only stars weighing between 1.4–3 Suns form neutron stars

At only 6–12 mi. (10–20km) across, I'm a tiny star, yet I weigh more than the Sun. My gravity is so immense that you'd have to reach half the speed of light in order to escape it. I spin at dizzying speeds, too—once every second isn't unusual. I'm made of neutrons that form when the electrons and protons of a supergiant join. Those of us detected from our alien-like bleeping sounds are called pulsars.

Neutron Star

A teaspoon of neutron material would weigh one billion tons!

● Discoverer: Jocelyn Bell Burnell (1967)
● Nickname: Little Green Man
● Number in the Milky Way: more than 2,000

Black Hole

All-Star Crew

* A hole in the fabric of space
* This secretive character hides by giving off no light radiation
* Only stars heavier than three Suns form black holes

Black Hole

Born out of the wreckage of a dying superstar, I am silent and deadly. My black heart forms when the core of a massive star collapses. With such powerful gravity, I destroy matter itself, shattering neutrons into subatomic particles until I shrink to a tiny point. Black holes are black because even light cannot escape from our deadly grasp. We warp space-time around us.

* Size: 10–15 times the Sun's mass
* Temperature: 180 million °F (100 million °C)
* Detected by: gamma-ray emissions

Anything falling into a black hole gets spaghettified!

Supernova Remnant

All-Star Crew

* The remains of a supernova (gas and dust blasted into space)
* The major source of cosmic rays in our galaxy
* Ever-expanding clouds that look like electric storms

Out of my way! I'm a screaming banshee crackling with energy! Traveling at speeds of up to 6.2 million mph (10 million km/h), my supernova remnant friends and I are unstoppable waves blasting from megapowerful supernova explosions. With fearsome 90,000°F (50,000°C) temperatures, our superheated plasma tears through space, giving off x-rays, cosmic rays, and all the pretty colors of a rainbow.

Fleeing the crime scene, we carry away almost the entire booty of a heavy star. Mature stars are packed full of heavier elements (carbon, oxygen, sodium, magnesium, sulfur, and iron), so we're responsible for populating the universe with the stuff necessary for life. Pretty hot, huh?

Travels at a breakneck one percent of the speed of light

* Famous SNR: Crab nebula (M1)
* Average SNR weight: 1×10^{28} tons
* Hottest SNR: 1.8 million °F (1 million °C)

Supernova Remnant

CHAPTER 6
Local Group

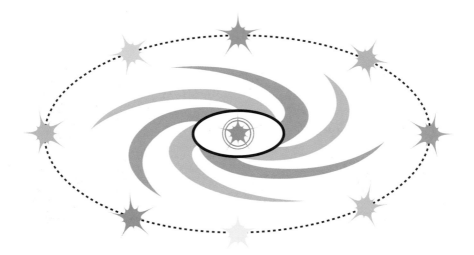

This posse of chiefs lords it over everyone, and everything about them is huge. We are talking galaxies—gigantic collections of billions of stars. Galaxies dwarf anything in our imagination, yet from afar they look like dim, fuzzy clouds compared with the closer stars inside the Milky Way. These galaxies sit behind the scenes, pulling the strings, as they rule space and time. Their colossal gravity means that they are found in clusters. The Local Group is our cluster—it has more than 40 galaxies in a volume of space measuring ten million light-years across.

The Milky Way

Supermassive
Black Hole

Magellanic Clouds

Andromeda Galaxy

Triangulum Galaxy

SETI

The Milky Way

■ Local Group

* A 13.7-billion-year-old galaxy, where humans live
* A spiral home to up to 500 billion stars
* Has four arms: Perseus, Cygnus, Centaurus, Sagittarius

Hanging in space like a gigantic pinwheel, I am The Galaxy—the only one that truly matters! I'm the place that your Sun and billions of other stars call home. I'm mind-twistingly massive—100,000 light-years wide—and the Sun takes 225 million years to go around me just once.

With the Sun buried snugly inside the Orion arm (a branch of the Sagittarius arm), your view of my huge central bulge is blocked. However, on dark nights, its glare is enough to make a pale stripe of stars across Earth's sky. My lovely big belly is crammed with red and yellow stars, which make me look like a fried egg—no "yolk"! Buzzing around in a halo are tight bunches of ancient stars called globular clusters, which often collide to form superhot blue stragglers. But my center also hides a dark secret . . .

It gets its name from looking like a trickle of spilled milk in Earth's sky.

● Galaxy type: barred spiral
● Size: 100,000 ly across
● Thickness: 1,000 ly

The Milky Way

Supermassive Black Hole

* A sleeping monster at the heart of the Milky Way galaxy
* This beast has the strongest force of gravity in the universe
* At its core, time stops and the laws of physics no longer apply

Pitch-black and still withholding my secrets from scientists, I'm the dark heart of a galaxy. I have a furious temper and a powerful appetite. Not even radiation can escape me—I eat up light for breakfast!

In the Milky Way, a mature galaxy, I've vacuumed my surroundings clean, leaving a bald patch around the middle. My massive cargo of star systems slowly circles me, while I play lord of the dance at the center. In the youngest galaxies far away, other SMBHs reveal their dark sides. They make distant galaxies flash frantically as they violently rip apart the stars that spiral into their gaping mouths and then burp out huge fountains of antimatter.

The SMBH in the Milky Way weighs as much as two million Suns!

- Milky Way's SMBH: Sagittarius A*
- Distance from Earth: 26,000 ly
- Number of SMBHs discovered: more than 30

Supermassive Black Hole

Magellanic Clouds

Local Group

* A pair of galactic large (LMC) and small (SMC) hangers-on
* LMC is in the constellation of Dorado, and SMC is in Tucana
* Both dwarf galaxies enjoy a great view of the Milky Way

We are a pair of beautiful filmy clouds adorning the Milky Way like a pair of lustrous sparkly earrings. We were named after Portuguese explorer Ferdinand Magellan, who was the first European to record our existence.

From Earth, we look like wispy blobs, but we most certainly are not! LMC weighs more than ten billion Suns and shines as brightly as two billion Suns. Astronomers thought that we were the Milky Way's closest companions, but they've since found the Sagittarius dwarf elliptical galaxy. We're a bit of an unknown—no one's sure whether we orbit the Milky Way or not. Astronomers even think that the thick clouds around our galactic interiors hide other galaxies.

They are visible with the naked eye from Earth's Southern Hemisphere.

* SMC distance to Milky Way: 210,000 ly
* Distance between clouds: 75,000 ly
* Brightest LMC supernova: 1987A

Magellanic Clouds

Andromeda Galaxy

■ Local Group

✳ An unfriendly neighbor in the constellation of Andromeda
✳ A big bully that's also called M31 or NGC 224

I'm the largest galaxy in the Local Group. Half as big as the Milky Way, I have more than one trillion stars. Who's the daddy? With your galaxy only 20 Milky-Way widths away, I'm a little too close for comfort, and I'm heading on a collision course with it! But don't be alarmed— the impact will be a soft merging of both of us and is not due for another five billion years.

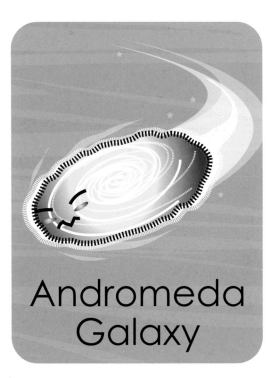

Andromeda Galaxy

The most distant object we can see with the naked eye

● Galaxy type: spiral
● Size: 250,000 ly across
● Light-years from Milky Way: 2.9 million

Triangulum Galaxy

Local Group ■

* ✻ A little beauty found in the constellation of Triangulum
* ✻ This baby galaxy cozies up to the Andromeda galaxy

Triangulum Galaxy

Andromeda, the Milky Way, and I are the Three Musketeers of the Local Group. Handsome and dashing, we contain 95 percent of all the matter in our big neighborhood. My fine-looking face is turned toward the Milky Way, so you have a lovely, clear view of my spiral structure. I also have one of the largest-known star-forming areas buried in my long, wispy arms.

* ● Galaxy type: spiral
* ● Size: around 60,000 ly across
* ● Light-years from Milky Way: 2.9 million

Traveling to our closest galaxy is still a thing of science fiction!

SETI
■ Local Group

* On a **S**earch for **E**xtra**T**errestrial **I**ntelligence
* An Earth-based project, putting a phone tap on ET
* Began in the swinging '60s and is now a worldwide quest

You might say I'm a bit of a hopeless task, but I could be the answer to humankind's most important question. Are Earthlings alone, or is there anything else alive out there? I'm a dragnet trawling the depths of space to catch signs of intelligent life. When there's a lot of noise coming from Earth, it makes sense to listen for the buzz of another civilization.

Scientists have sent text messages from the world's most powerful radio telescopes and have scanned the sky with radio and optical receivers. But in many decades of tuning in to the static from outer space, I've heard barely a peep. So there continues to be one big unknown: is the universe crawling with life on millions of alien "Earths," or is your planet truly special and one of a kind?

SETI@home is the world's second-fastest computer.

* First SETI search: Frank Drake (1960)
* Possible signal: Wow! signal (1977)
* Detected by: Big Ear radio telescope

SETI

CHAPTER 7
Deep Space Gang

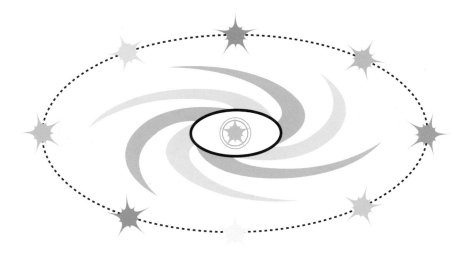

Galaxies in the Deep Space Gang come in three classes: spiral (like the Milky Way), elliptical, and irregular. There are trillions of galaxies in the universe, but the distances between these enormous families of stars are so eye-wateringly incomprehensible that each galaxy is like an island in the vastness of space. This posse of far-out freaks holds the key to the universe's deepest mysteries. The shapes they make tell a story about the conditions of the universe when it came into being, and they also give us clues about its final destiny.

Virgo Supercluster

Elliptical Galaxy

Active Galaxy

Colliding Galaxies

Hubble Space Telescope

Red Shift

Virgo Supercluster
■ Deep Space Gang

- ☀ A large pattern in the universe, millions of light-years wide
- ☀ A structure containing thousands and thousands of galaxies
- ☀ Virgo cluster is the largest group for 50 million light-years around

Your Local Group lies on my outskirts. Groups of galaxies huddle together in clusters, and in turn, these different clusters can be clumped together into superclusters. I am your local supercluster, and right in the middle is the aggressive Virgo cluster.

These guys in the Virgo cluster are the biggest, baddest gang in the supercluster—the older boys who dominate the 'hood. (Astronomers can tell the age of a galaxy by how many collisions it has had, how trashed its spiral arms look, and how elliptical it is.) With around 150 big bruiser galaxies and more than 2,000 dwarf galaxies, the Virgo cluster's gravity tugs on all the other groups around.

The Local Group is tumbling into the Virgo cluster at around 155 mi. (250km)/s!

- ● Size: 200 million ly across
- ● Mass: one quadrillion Suns
- ● Number of groups and clusters: more than 100

Virgo Supercluster

Elliptical Galaxy
■ Deep Space Gang

✴ Huge squished ball of old stars, starved of star-making gases
✴ Beanlike bulge that has stopped making new stars
✴ About 10–15 percent of Local Group galaxies are elliptical

I'm more demure than the fancy-pants spiral galaxies like the Milky Way with their floppy, swinging arms. Some people think that I look like a shapeless blob, but that overlooks my exquisite structure—I'm more like a bean-shaped pod of old red stars. I also take life at a slower pace than those hectic spirals. Their stars race around frantically, while mine orbit my center at a more sedate pace.

Elliptical galaxies come in all sizes, from dwarfs to giants. Dwarfs are the original galaxies, formed from the first clouds of gas in the universe. They're petite and hard to spot in the night sky, yet they outnumber all the universe's other galaxies. Giant ellipticals are rarer and are even hefty enough to affect the gravity of a supercluster. One thing we all share is a lack of material to form new stars.

The Sagittarius dwarf elliptical galaxy is the closest one to the Milky Way.

● Shape: ball- or egg-shaped
● Largest: one million ly across
● Smallest: one tenth of the Milky Way

Elliptical Galaxy

Active Galaxy
■ Deep Space Gang

✳ A supercharged galaxy with an inner demon
✳ Radio telescopes tune in to listen to its torments
✳ Supermassive black holes tear the heart out of this poor soul

Unpredictable galaxies like me let everyone know how unhappy we are. Deep within me is a supermassive black hole in a bad mood. Its terrible fury unleashes the most energetic storms in the universe—screaming jets of radio waves and x-rays as gamma rays erupt in fountains above and below my flat galactic disk. With all this howling, I'm heard throughout space.

Active Galaxy

Most quasars are more than ten billion light-years away.

● Discoverer: Carl Keenan Seyfert (1943)
● Types: Seyfert, quasar, blazar, and radio
● Also known as: active galactic nucleus

Colliding Galaxies

Deep Space Gang ■

* The result of two galaxies crashing into each other
* Middle-aged hefties with a fatal attraction to each other
* The Andromeda galaxy is headed straight for the Milky Way

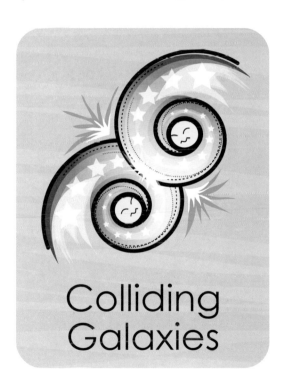

Colliding Galaxies

We're the biggest "crunch" you'll ever see. Lumbering galaxies weighing many millions of Suns sometimes smash into each other. Drawn toward each other by their huge gravity, the outcome is inevitable. It's a car accident in the sky! The force of the impact makes us turn cartwheels and form lovely spiral arms. Then, after a burst of star birth, all the gas is driven off.

● Merging galaxy: Arp 273
● Collision speed: up to 185 mi. (300km)/s
● Average time to merge: one billion years

Without gas, old galaxies look blobby and don't make new stars.

Hubble Space Telescope

■ Deep Space Gang

✱ A blurry-eyed telescope that became a hero of astronomy
✱ HST can see in ultraviolet, infrared, and visible frequencies
✱ Can focus on a tiny blip of light millions of light-years away

Hubba-hubba. I'm a complete hunk! Flying in low-Earth orbit and shaped like a flip-top trash can the size of a school bus, I've been sent to take snapshots of space without any background light or pesky atmospheric wobbles.

My beady eye has spied stuff all around the Milky Way, but I've made my name by looking outside the galaxy. Peering into the depths of space, I've been able to look back in time, because light takes many, many years to travel from distant galaxies. By capturing light from galaxies 13 billion light-years away—the farthest ever seen—I've shown astronomers the universe as it looked that long ago. I'm the original time-traveling hero!

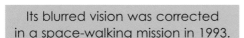

Its blurred vision was corrected in a space-walking mission in 1993.

● Originator: Lyman Spitzer (1914–1997)
● Orbiting height: 366 mi. (589km)
● Time taken to orbit Earth: 97 minutes

Hubble Space Telescope

Red Shift
Deep Space Gang

✳ A bigwig concept that proves the universe is getting larger
✳ This runaway guy makes whizzing galaxies look redder
✳ Used as a measurement of distance for really far-off galaxies

I'm a mind-bender. I scare the pants off people because I seem so brain-frizzlingly complicated, but I'm one of the most important ideas in astronomy—stay with me and I'll explain why. In much the same way as a police car's siren changes in pitch when it passes you, light coming from moving stars and galaxies can shift in frequency, too.

Because most of the Deep Space Gang are traveling away from Earth, light coming from them is shifted toward red (lower-frequency) light—that is, they look redder than they actually are. Red shift—geddit? It gets better. Galaxies that are farther away are traveling faster and have more of me, so I can be used as a measurement of distance for objects in space—so the more red shift, the farther away something is.

Hubble used red shift to figure out that everything is traveling away from us.

● Discoverer: Christian Doppler (1842)
● First used in astronomy: Armand Fizeau (1848)
● Largest red shift: 96% of light speed

Red Shift

CHAPTER 8
The Universals

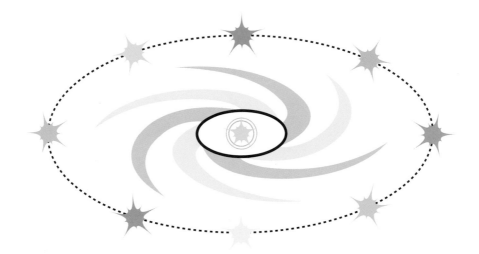

This strange crew underpins the universe—they help tell us how it all began, govern the shape of everything, and determine how it grows older. They are the driving forces behind our 13.7-billion-year-old cosmos, and since space is 99.9999 percent nothing, they know that things made of matter are very insignificant. The Universals are a bewilderingly clever bunch, and by understanding them, we can begin to answer mind-boggling questions—such as what is the universe, where did it come from, and is there anything at all outside it?

The Big Bang

WMAP

Dark Matter

Dark Energy

Space-time

The Big Bang

The Universals

- ☀ The best theory of how the universe was created
- ☀ A 13.7-billion-year-old blast from the past, it's pals with Red Shift
- ☀ This motivated self-starter explains why the universe is expanding

Old, mystical, and unknowable, I am the start of time itself. I am the beginning of everything. Chapter one. Page one. At first there was nothing. And then, in fractions of a second, I created all matter, energy, and order.

Scientists can only speculate about what triggered me, but I exploded into life in a burst of energy and exotic particles. My "big bang" spawned a blazing ball of fundamental particles, true to Albert Einstein's famous equation $E = mc^2$ (which shows how energy can be converted into matter). Later on, these particles would cool and clump together to form atoms, molecules, and the beginnings of the stars and galaxies that we see today. The energy was enough to blow the universe wide open to its current, almost immeasurable, size. And it's still expanding.

At the start, the universe doubled in size in under one trillionth of a second!

- ● Discoverer: Georges Lemaître (1927)
- ● Initial temperature: 1×10^{34}°C
- ● Radiation mapped by: *COBE* satellite

The Big Bang

WMAP
The Universals

✳ Has the handsome title **W**ilkinson **M**icrowave **A**nisotropy **P**robe
✳ A shiny toy that measures the glow of the universe's ancient heat
✳ Its breakthrough dated the big bang to 13.7 billion years ago

I'm a robot on a mission. I have been fired into space to measure any ripples in heat coming from the big bang. The cosmic microwave background (CMB) is the soft glow left over from the superhot explosion that kick-started the universe. It's all around us, coming from every direction. If we could see microwaves rather than visible light, the whole sky would be on fire. Even your TV picks up this cosmic hiss—one percent of the static on an untuned channel comes from the depths of space!

My job has been a little like sifting through the Sahara Desert to list every grain of sand that is a fraction bigger or smaller than the norm. Others would give up, but not me. I have mapped the all-important tiny irregularities (or "lumps"), which gave rise to the galaxies of today's universe.

CMB comes from a time 400,000 years after the big bang.

● Discoverers (CMB): Arno Penzias, Robert Wilson
● Average temperature (CMB): −455°F (−270°C)
● Launch date (WMAP): June 30, 2001

WMAP

Dark Matter
The Universals

* A big chunk of matter in the universe is made from this fellow
* Could be a new type of matter or a version of ordinary matter
* A map of this dastardly elusive guy was made in 1997

They seek me here, they seek me there, those astronomers seek me everywhere. Cloaked from detection, I'm pretty much invisible. It's like playing a game of hide-and-seek in the fog! I don't interact with any form of light radiation, so I can't be seen on any of the frequencies used by astronomers to explore the universe—whether it's radio, microwave, infrared, visible light, ultraviolet, x-ray, or gamma ray.

Although I shy away from the limelight, I still pull on "ordinary matter" with my gravity, and it's this pull that gives me away. Wherever I am, galaxies spin faster than they would if they were just made of normal matter. I explain many weird things, including galaxies buzzing around too quickly or light warping around invisible objects!

Spiral galaxies spin so fast that they'd break apart without me.

* Discoverer: Fritz Zwicky (1898–1974)
* Percentage of universe: 23%
* Types: MACHOs, WIMPs, and neutrinos

Dark Matter

Dark Energy
The Universals

- Unexplained force, a partner in invisible crime with Dark Matter
- This strange energy floods the entire universe and pulls it apart
- Crucial in the first fractions of a second after the big bang

Full of deviltry and mischief, I am the master of all things dark! I am a type of antigravity pulling the strings behind the scenes—a silent force driving the universe apart. I'm probably the prime mover behind the universe's creation and am responsible for its ultimate destiny.

I was discovered when scientists looked at supernova explosions to try to find out whether the universe's expansion was slowing down. They were shocked to find that it was actually speeding up! The truth is that I am a huge embarrassment to Earth's astronomers, because even though they can see my effects, they are completely in the dark about what I am all about. You see, when astronomers don't really know much about something, they stick "dark" in front of its name—like my cousin, Dark Matter.

The universe is expanding by around 40 mi. (70km) every second.

- Discoverer: Michael Turner (1998)
- Percentage of universe: 73%
- Particles: act against gravity's pull

Dark Energy

Space-time

The Universals

* A 4-D beast and the wackiest member of the Universals
* Warps create gravity and can even bend light
* Is the very fabric of space itself

Welcome to the fourth dimension! I am a higher being all around you—the framework on which the universe is built—yet your puny human senses cannot perceive me. Because you're used to seeing in only three dimensions, you cannot even imagine what I look like.

In the wild wastes of space, time loses its steady ticktock. It runs slower for things traveling close to the speed of light and is also affected when it's close to heavy stuff like black holes. So supersmart astronomers build time into a fourth dimension along with the normal three dimensions of space: height, width, and depth. This allows scientists to describe events (like the orbits of far-off planets) rather than just positions and speeds— I provide a relative time and place for everything!

It warps around black holes so tightly that the laws of physics break down.

● Discoverer: Albert Einstein (1905)
● Theory: the theory of relativity
● The fourth dimension: time

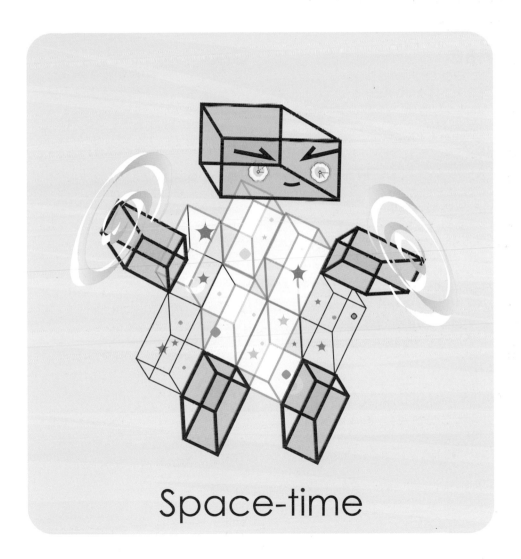

Space-time

INDEX

ABC
active galaxy 106
Alpha Centauri 66
Andromeda galaxy 96, 97, 107
asteroid belt 28
Betelgeuse 76
big bang 114, 116
black hole 82, 85, 122
brown dwarf 62, 64
Caloris basin 12
Cassini-Huygens 38
Cat's Eye Nebula 78
Charon 48
colliding galaxies 107
comets 18, 46, 53, 54
constellation 58, 66, 74, 76, 78, 94

DEF
dark energy 120
dark matter 118, 120
dwarf planets 8, 28, 46, 48, 49, 52
Earth 10, 16, 18, 19, 20, 22, 28
Einstein, Albert 114, 122
elliptical galaxy 104
Eris 46, 49, 52
extrasolar planet 68

GHI
galaxies 8, 88, 90, 92, 94, 96, 97, 100, 102, 104, 106, 107, 127
Galilei, Galileo 4, 34, 36
gas giants 28, 30, 32, 36, 42, 44, 51
Hale-Bopp 53
Halley's comet 54
Hubble space telescope 108
International Space Station 20

JKL
Jupiter 28, 32, 34, 51
Jupiter's moons 34
Kuiper belt 46, 50, 52, 54
Local Group 88–99, 102

MNO
Magellanic Clouds 94
main planets 6, 8, 12, 14, 16, 24, 30, 32, 36, 42, 44
Mars 24, 26
Mars rovers 24, 26
Mercury 12
meteorite 18, 34
Milky Way 8, 88, 90, 92, 94, 96, 97, 100

Moon 22
moons 8, 24, 32, 34, 36,
  38, 40, 49, 50, 51, 127
Neptune 44, 48, 52
neutron star 82, 84
New Horizons 46, 50
near Earth asteroids 28
Oort cloud 46, 53
open cluster 62

PQR
planets 6, 8, 12, 14, 16, 24,
  30, 32, 36, 42, 44, 48, 49,
  68, 98, 128
Pluto 46, 48, 50, 52
red dwarf 65
red shift 110

STU
Saturn 36, 38, 40, 51
SETI 98
Sirius 74
solar system 6–55
spacecraft 19, 20, 26,
  38, 40, 42, 46, 50, 51,
  108, 116
space junk 19
space-time 85, 122
star birth nebula 56, 60,
  62, 64, 82

stars 6, 8, 56–87, 90, 96, 97,
  104, 114, 128
Sun 6, 8, 22, 90
supergiant 62, 70, 82, 84
supermassive black hole
  92, 106
supernova 70, 76, 82, 84,
  86
supernova remnant 86
Titan 38, 40
Triangulum galaxy 97
universe 4, 112, 114, 116,
  118, 120, 122, 128
Uranus 42

VW
Venus 14
Virgo supercluster 102
Voyagers 46, 51
white dwarf 78, 80
WMAP 116

GLOSSARY

Absolute magnitude A star's true brightness in space.
Apparent magnitude A star's brightness as seen from Earth.
Asteroid A space rock orbiting the Sun, found mostly in the doughnut-shaped belt between Mars and Jupiter.
Astronaut A person who travels in space.
Astronomer A person who studies the universe.
Astronomical unit (au) A unit used to measure very large distances—1 au is the average distance between Earth and the Sun (93 million mi./149.6 million km).
Atmosphere A layer of gases surrounding a planet, moon, or star that is held in place by its gravity.
Axis An imaginary line that goes through the center of a planet or celestial body, around which it rotates.
Brightness A measurement of a star's light or total radiation given off each second. Also known as luminosity.
Celestial object Any object seen in the sky, whether a planet, star, or galaxy.
Core The central part of a star or planet.
Corona A superhot outer layer of gas around the Sun, visible as a halo during a total eclipse.
Crater A bowl-shaped hollow on the surface of a planet, moon, or asteroid, formed when a space rock crashes into it.
Crust A thin, rocky layer covering the surface of a planet or moon.
Eclipse When a celestial object moves into the shadow of another object, partially or fully obscuring it from view.

Elliptical orbit An oval shaped path.

Galaxy A vast family of stars, gas, and dust held together by gravity.

Gravity A force of attraction between objects.

Greenhouse effect The rising temperatures in Earth's atmosphere caused by the buildup of carbon dioxide, methane, and other gases.

Lava Molten rock that flows from a planet's center.

Light-year (ly) A unit of distance—1 ly is the distance light travels in one year (5.88 trillion mi./9.46 trillion km).

Local Group A cluster of galaxies and the home of the Milky Way.

Magnetic field A region of space around a planet or star where magnetism extends.

Meteor A streak of light produced by a meteoroid as it travels through Earth's atmosphere and burns up. Also called a shooting star.

Moon A natural satellite orbiting a planet or asteroid.

NASA The National Aeronautics and Space Administration of the United States.

Nuclear fusion A reaction that takes place inside a star, releasing huge amounts of energy.

Observatory A building that houses telescopes.

Orbit The path that one object takes around another, more massive object. The Moon orbits Earth.

Photosphere The visible surface layer of a star.

GLOSSARY

Planet A large, round body made of rock or gas that orbits a star.

Ring system A collection of rings around a planet made up of dust, rock, and ice.

Satellite An object held in orbit around a planet or moon by gravity. The Moon is a natural satellite, and a space telescope is an example of a human-made satellite.

Solar wind A stream of invisible particles blown out from the Sun into space.

Space probe A crewless spacecraft sent to explore the solar system and beyond.

Space station A large human-made satellite orbiting Earth where astronauts can live and perform scientific experiments over fairly long periods.

Spaghettification The stretching of objects in space into long, thin shapes. This happens near black holes.

Spin One complete rotation of a celestial object on its axis.

Star A ball of hot, bright gas that produces energy by a nuclear reaction.

Stellar Of or like a star.

Tilt The angle at which an axis is leaning.

Universe Everything that exists—all of space and everything it contains.